STRUCTURAL ENGINEERING DIPLOMA & ENGINEERING MCQ

MANOJ DOLE

Made with ♥ on the Notion Press Platform
www.notionpress.com

Contents

Foreword

Structural Engineering Diploma & Engineering MCQ is a simple Book for Structural Diploma & Engineering Course, It contains objective questions with underlined & bold correct answers MCQ covering all topics including all about the latest & Important about Fundamentals of Engineering Drawings, Construction and Civil Engineering Technology, Structural Fundamentals, Soils and Foundations, Fluid Mechanics and Hydraulics, Structural Analysis, Structural Design of Concrete, Structural Design of Steel, Advanced Structural Design, Design and Computing, Structural Engineering Design Project and lots more.

We add new question answers with each new version. Please email us in case of any errors/omissions. This is arguably the largest and best Book for All engineering multiple choice questions and answers.

As a student you can use it for your exam prep. This Book is also useful for professors to refresh material.

Preface

This book may be purchased for educational, business, or sales promotional use. Online edition is also available for this title. For more information, contact our corporate/institutional sales department: [+919921582799] or [manojdole1@gmail.com]

While every precaution has been taken in the preparation of this book, the publisher and authors assume no responsibility for errors or omissions, or for damages resulting from the use of the information contained herein.

About the Author

MANOJ DOLE is an Engineer from reputed University. He is currently working with Government Industrial Training- Institute as a lecturer from last 12 Years. His interest include- Engineering Training Material, Invention & Engineering Practical- Knowledge etc.

CHAPTER ONE

Structural Engineering Hand Tools & Measuring Instruments Theory

Download App
Online Test Exam
ITI Books
AutoCAD CAM
JOB & Apprentice
Online Theory
Computer Course
Trading Course
CNC Course
MSCIT Course
Shopping Business
Internet Business
Web Designing
Online Services
Top Sportsmans
Indian Army
Freedom Fighters
Top Scientists
Social Reformers
Motivational Speaker
Top Richest People
Join WhatsApp Group
Join Facebook Group
Like Facebook Page
PAN / Adhar / Licence
Passport

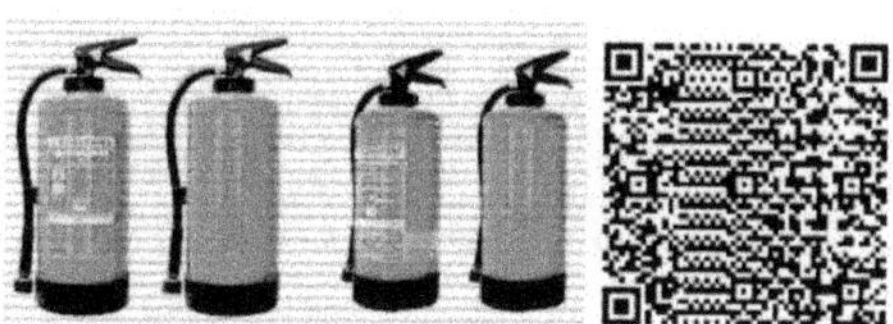

Fire extinguisher

Calliper

Hacksaw frame

Universal surface guage

Hammer

Centre punch

Bench vice

Files

Scraper

Surface Plate

Outside Micrometer

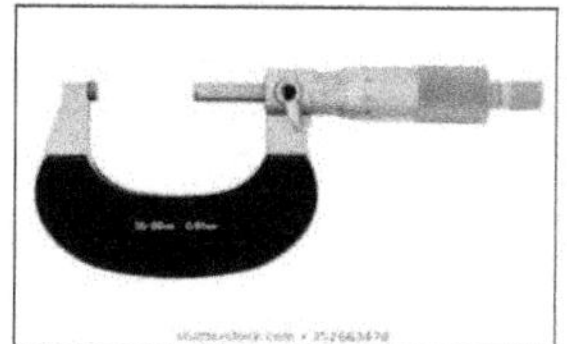

Micrometer

Depth micrometer

Vernier Calliper

Vernier bevel protractor

Drilling

Reamer

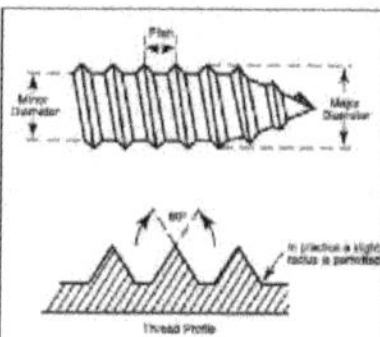 

Thread

Tap Die

Grinding Wheel

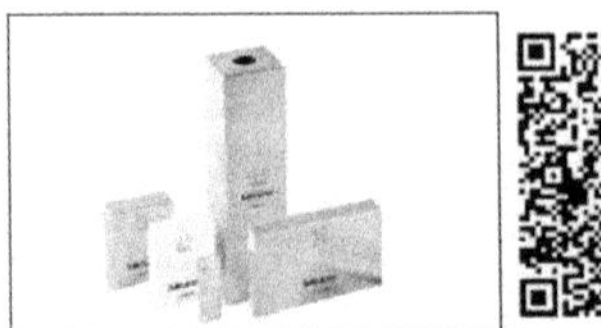

Slip gauge

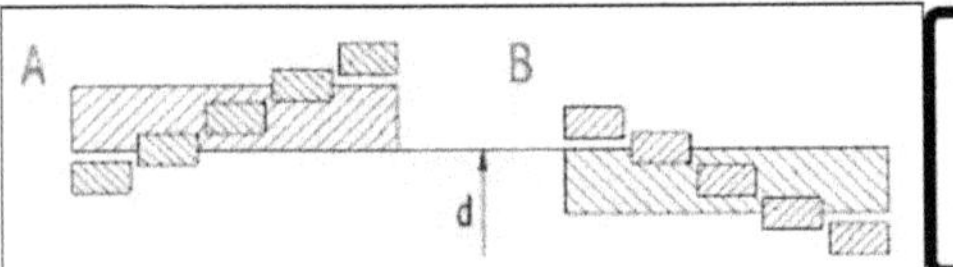

Limit fit tolerance

Lathe Machine

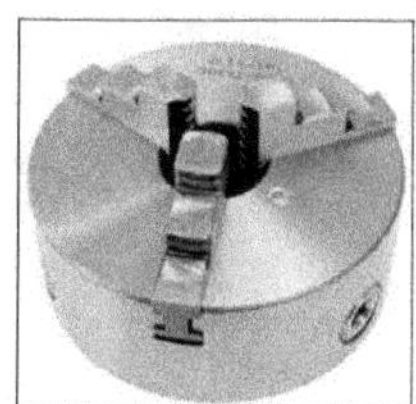

Lathe chuck

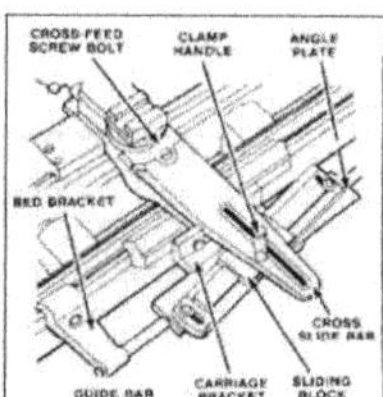

Taper turning attachment

taper ring gauge

screw pitch gauge

Gear

screw pitch gauge

Tap Die

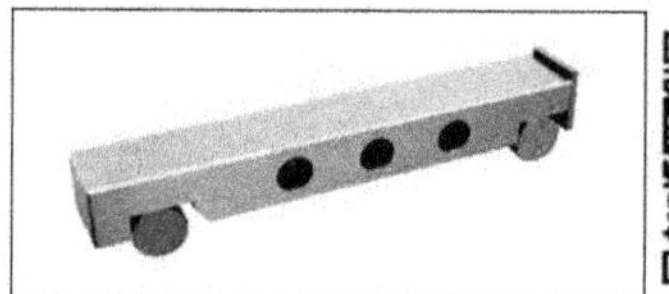

Sine bar

Slip gauge

Dial test indicator

Telescopic gauge

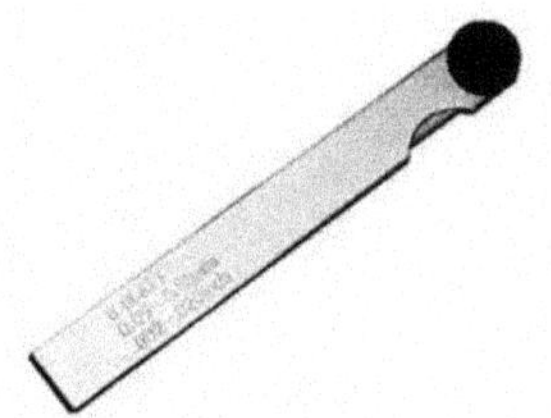

Feeler gauge

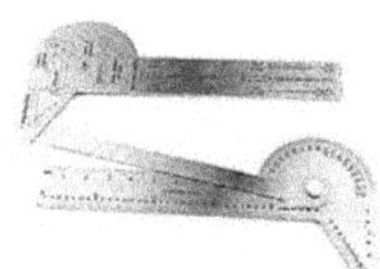

Centre gauge

Jig

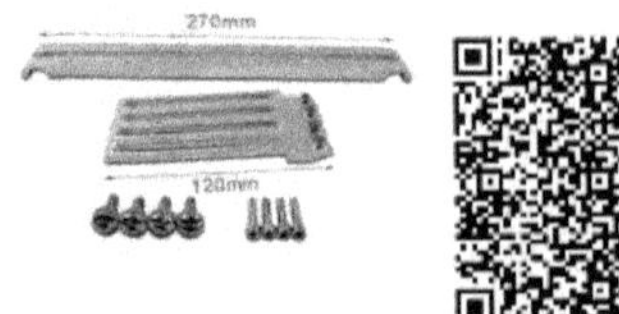

Fixture

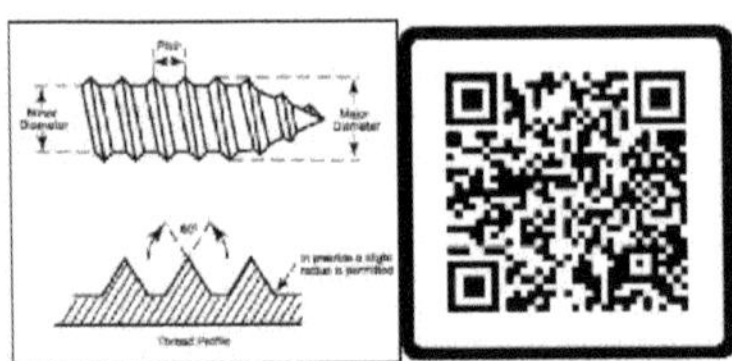

Thread

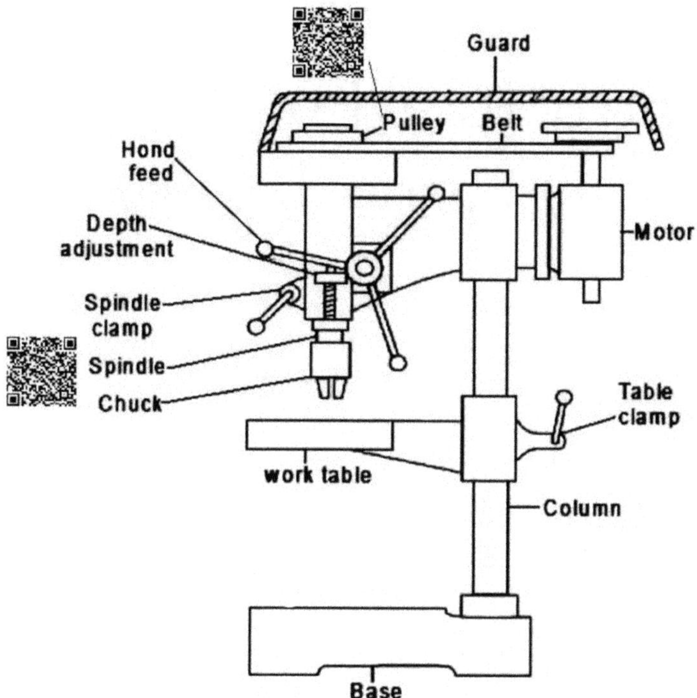

Piller Drilling Machine

CHAPTER TWO

Structural Engineering Drawing Theory

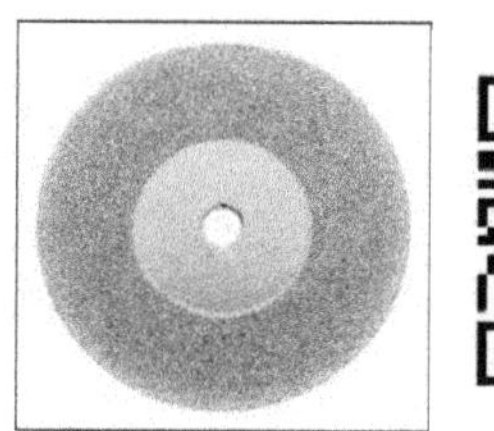

Grinding

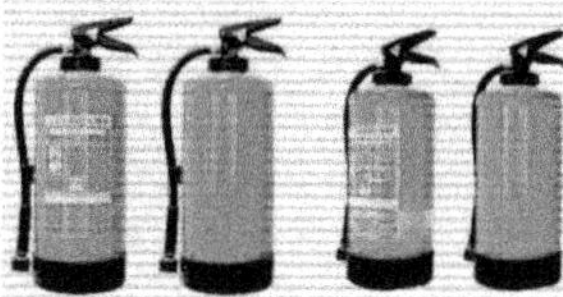

Fire extinguisher

French curve in drawing

Set square in drawing

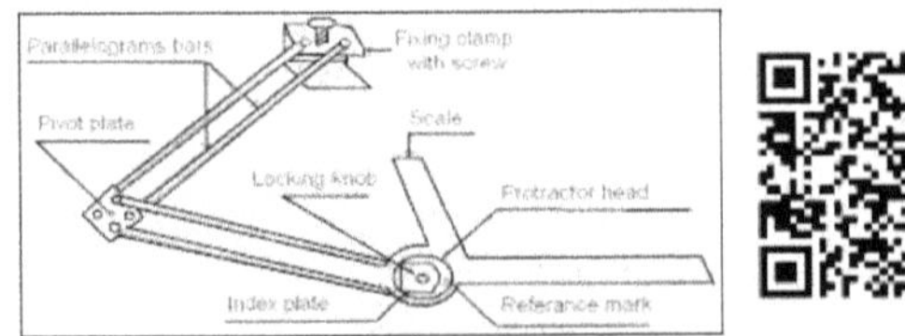

Mini drafter in drawing

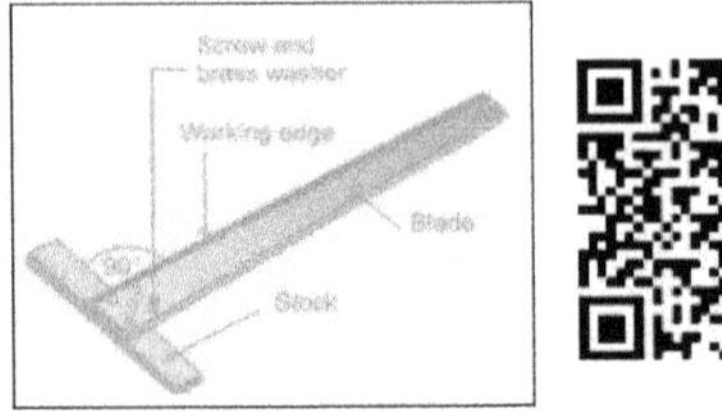

T - square in drawing

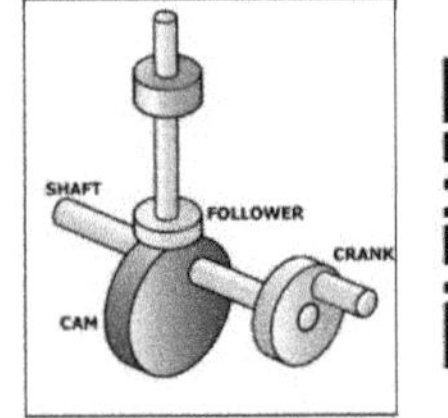

Cams in engine

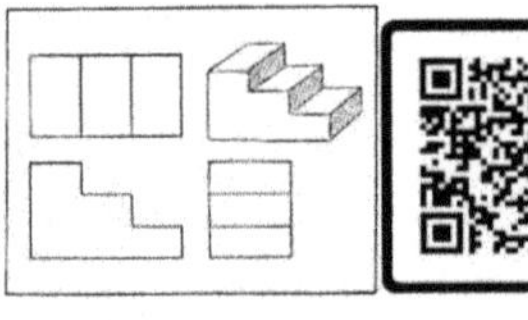

Orthographic projection in drawing

Third angle projection drawing

Cone in engineering drawing

Sphere in drawing

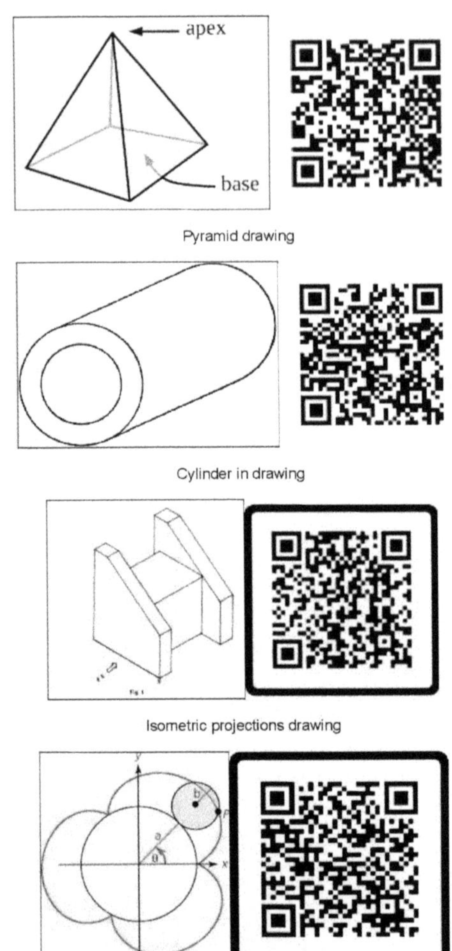

Pyramid drawing

Cylinder in drawing

Isometric projections drawing

Curves engineering drawing

Sectional views in drawing

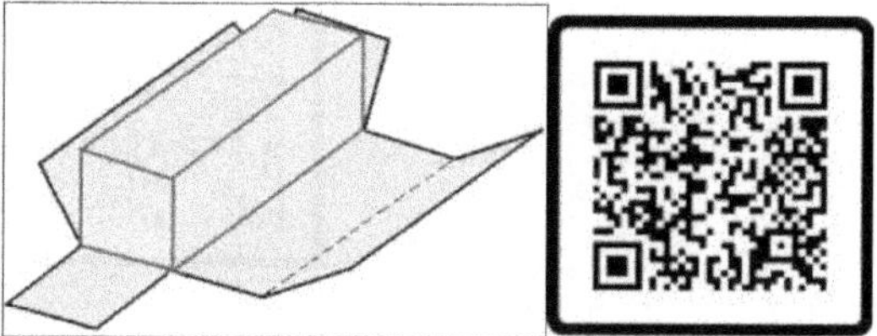

Development of surfaces in drawing

Hexagonal plane in drawing

Polyhedron in drawing

First Angle projection method in drawing

Springs in drawing

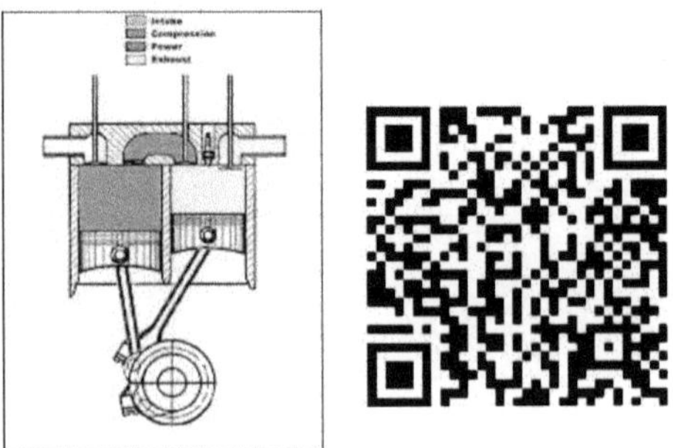

Engine in vehicle

CHAPTER THREE

Structural Engineering Hydraulic System & Pnumatic System Theory

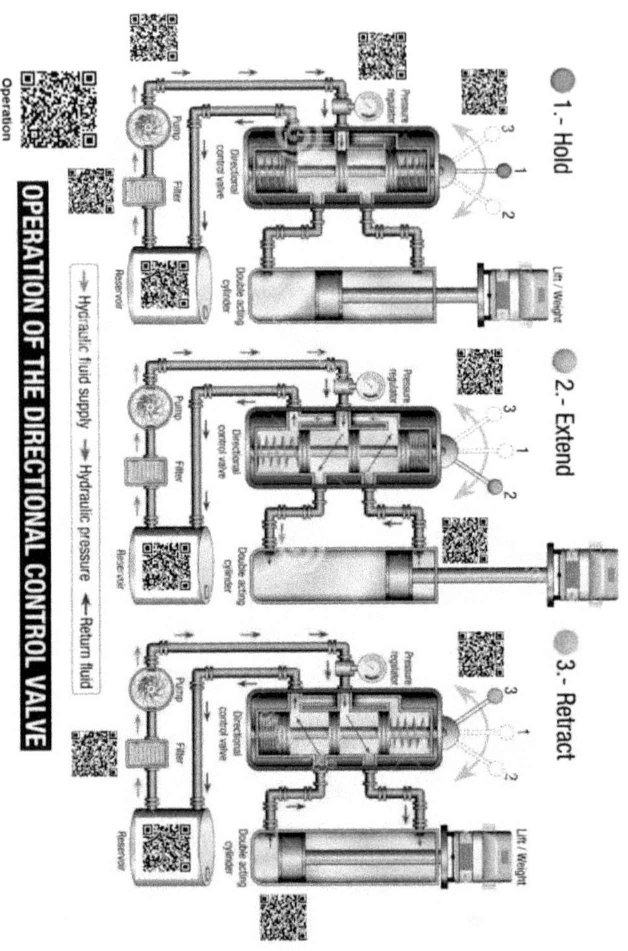
1.- Hold
2.- Extend
3.- Retract
Pressure regulator
Pump
Filter
Directional control valve
Double acting cylinder
Reservoir
Lift / Weight
Hydraulic fluid supply
Hydraulic pressure
Return fluid
Operation
OPERATION OF THE DIRECTIONAL CONTROL VALVE

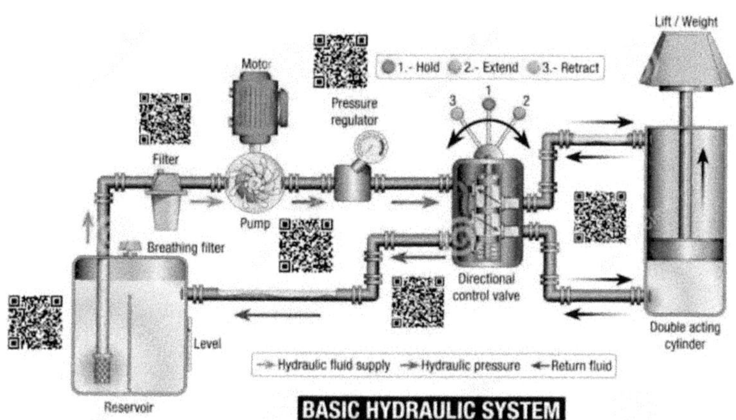

Direct Pressure Relief Valves

- The pressure relief valve provides protection against overload experienced by the actuators in a hydraulic system. One important function is to limit the force or torque produced by the hydraulic cylinders or motors.

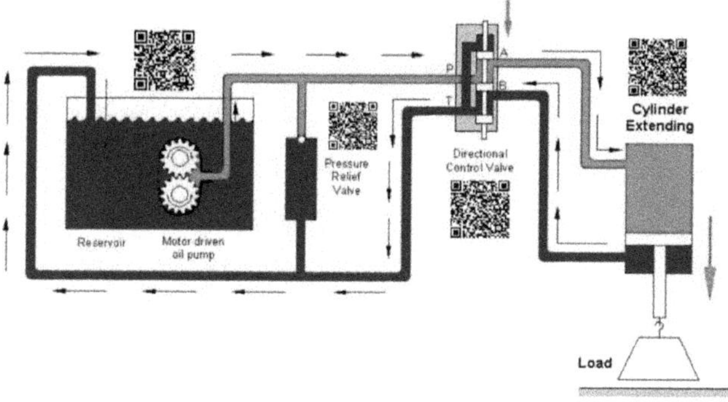

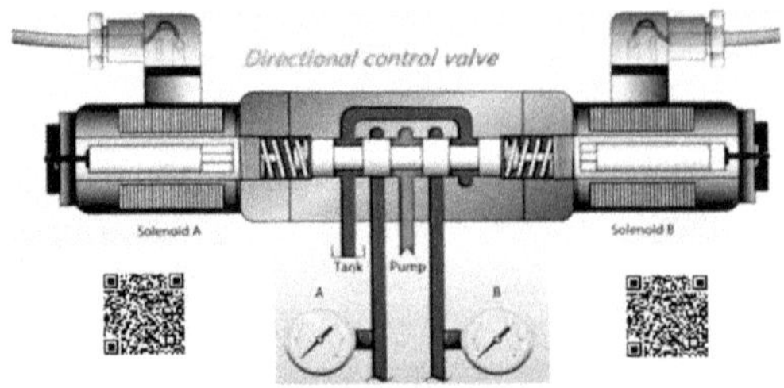

Double Acting, Single ended Cylinder

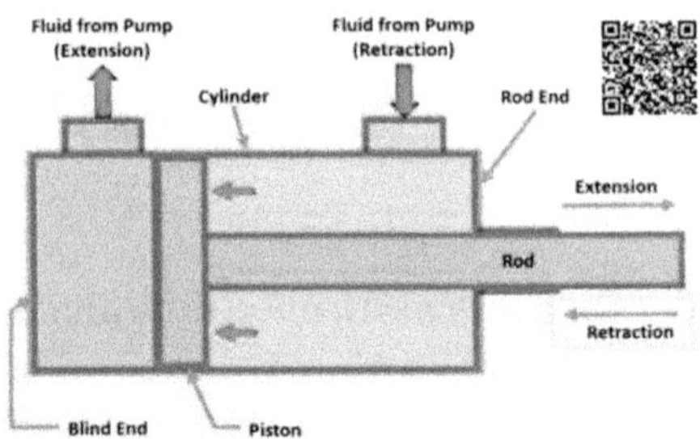

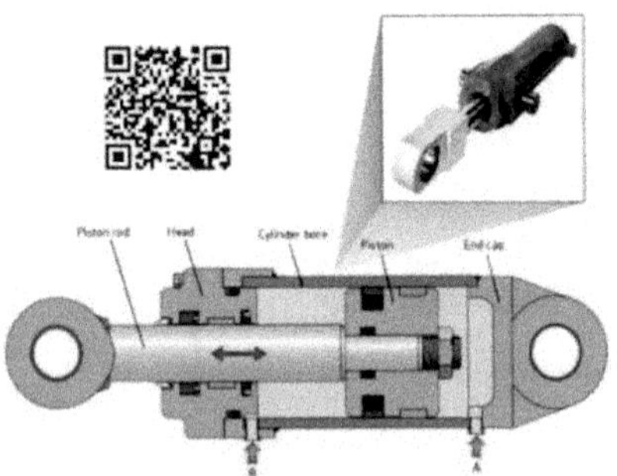

Hydraulic Cylinder

FLOW CONTROL VALVES

- A flow control valve can regulate the flow or pressure of the fluid.
- The fluid flow is controlled by varying area of the valve opening through which fluid passes.

GLOBE VALVE BUTTERFLY VALVE PLUG VALVE

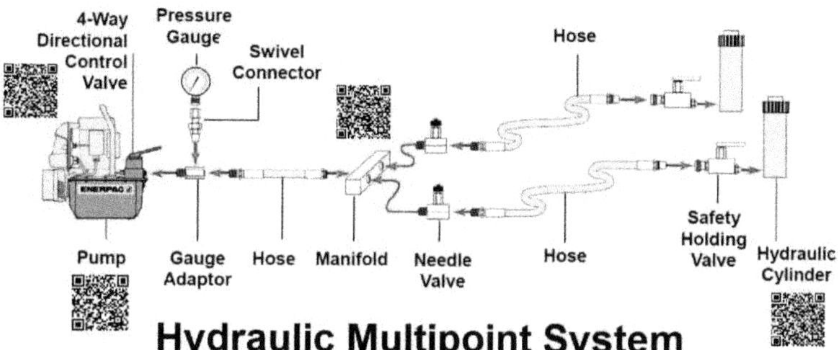

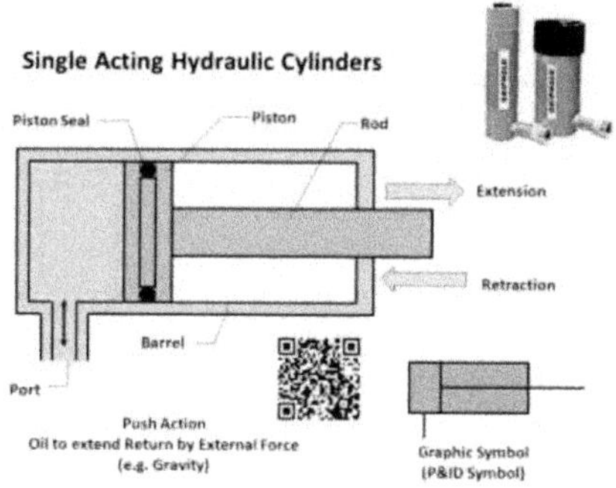

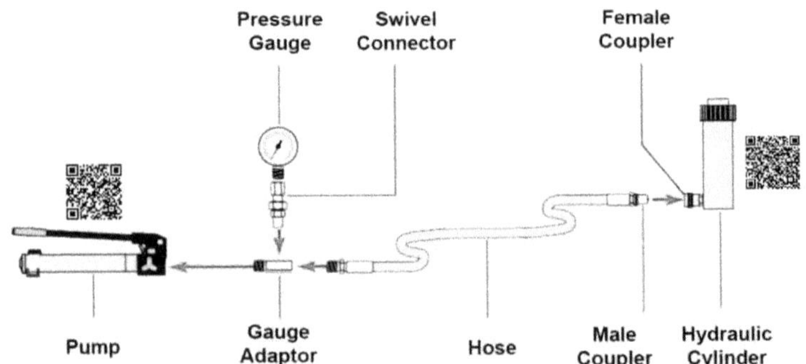

Hydraulic Single Point System

Types of Hydraulic Valves

- **Directional Control Valve:**

  Control the direction of flow of the hydraulic fluid to different lines in the circuit

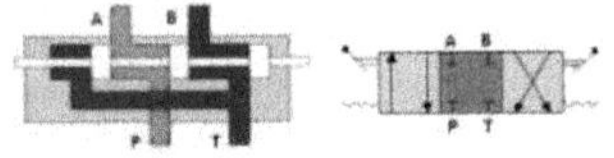

- **Flow Control Valves:**

  Control the amount of fluid flow in the circuit

- **Pressure Control Valves:**

  Control the pressure in different segments in the circuit

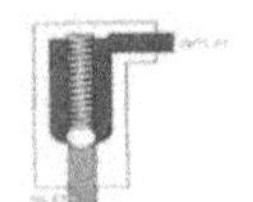

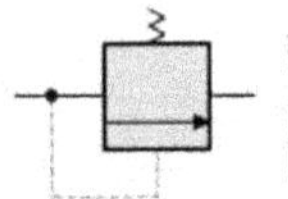

Hydraulic Valves - Parts and Components

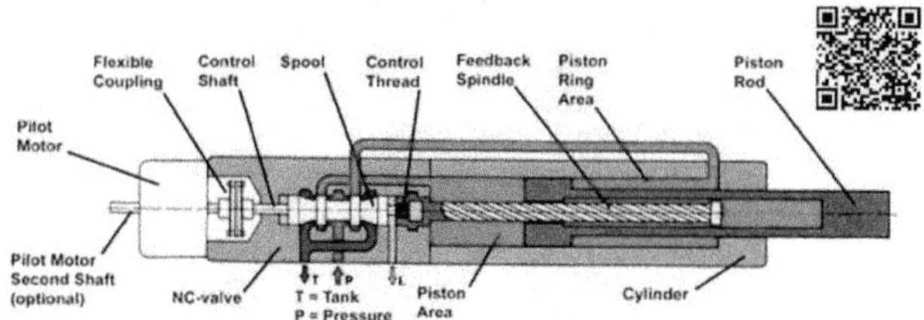

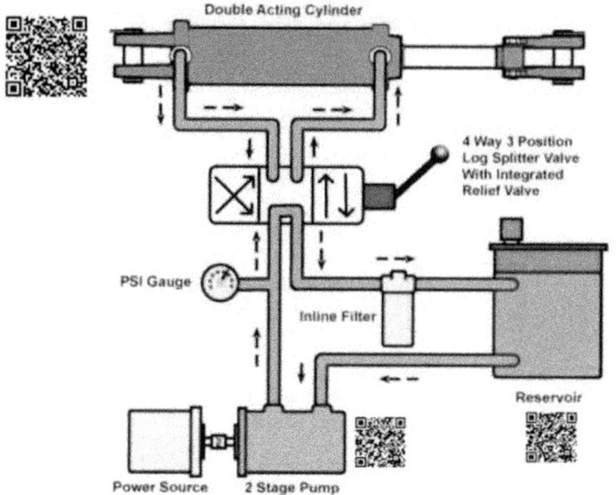

Hydraulic Double Acting Cylinder

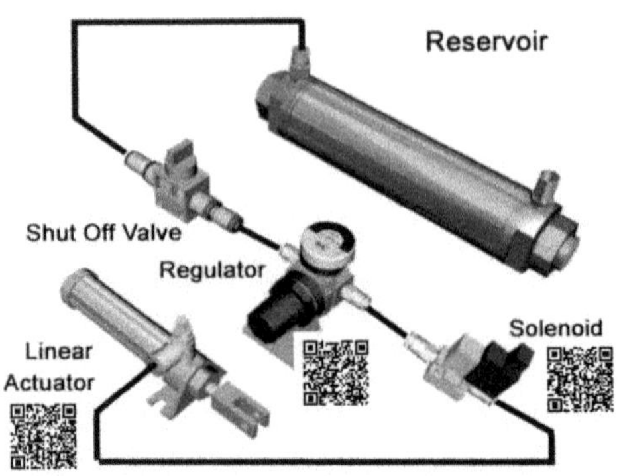

Pneumatic System

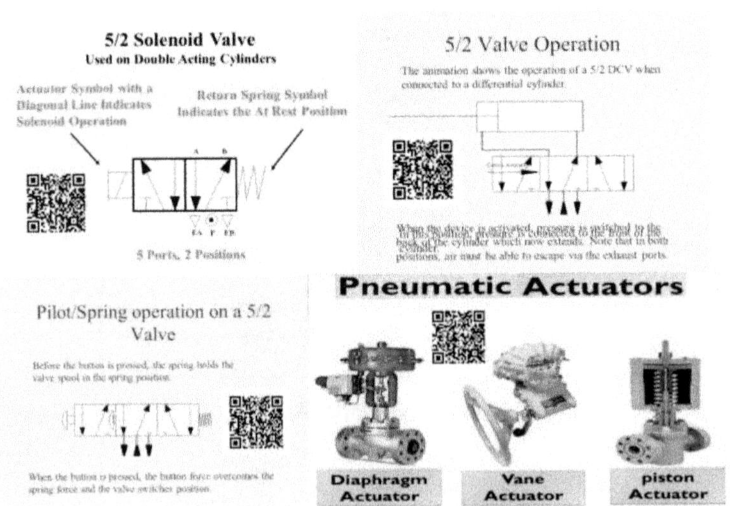

Pneumatic Control Valve **Pneumatic Control Valve Mechanisem**

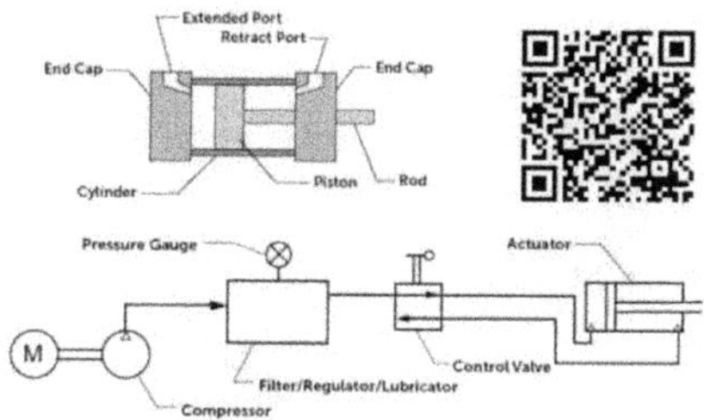

Pneumatic Cylinder System

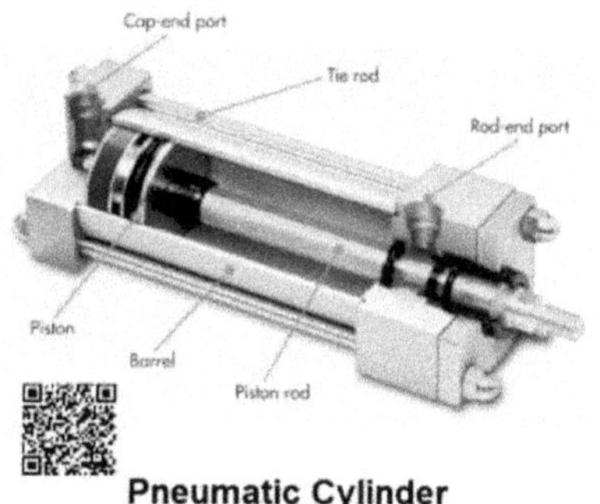

Pneumatic Cylinder

Pneumatic Cylinder

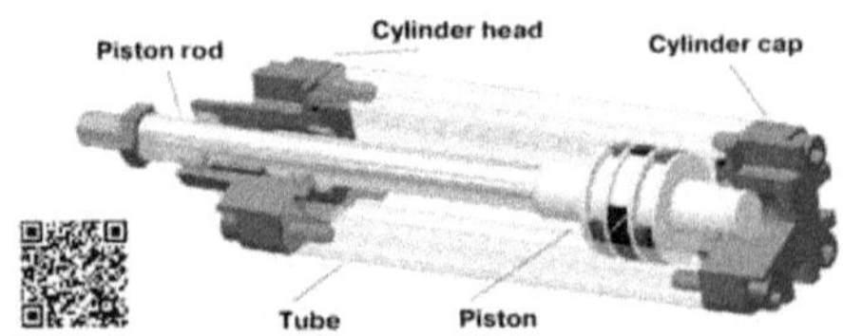

2-way, 2-position, normally closed direct-acting solenoid valve, spring return

4-way (5-port), 2-position, piloted solenoid valve, spring return

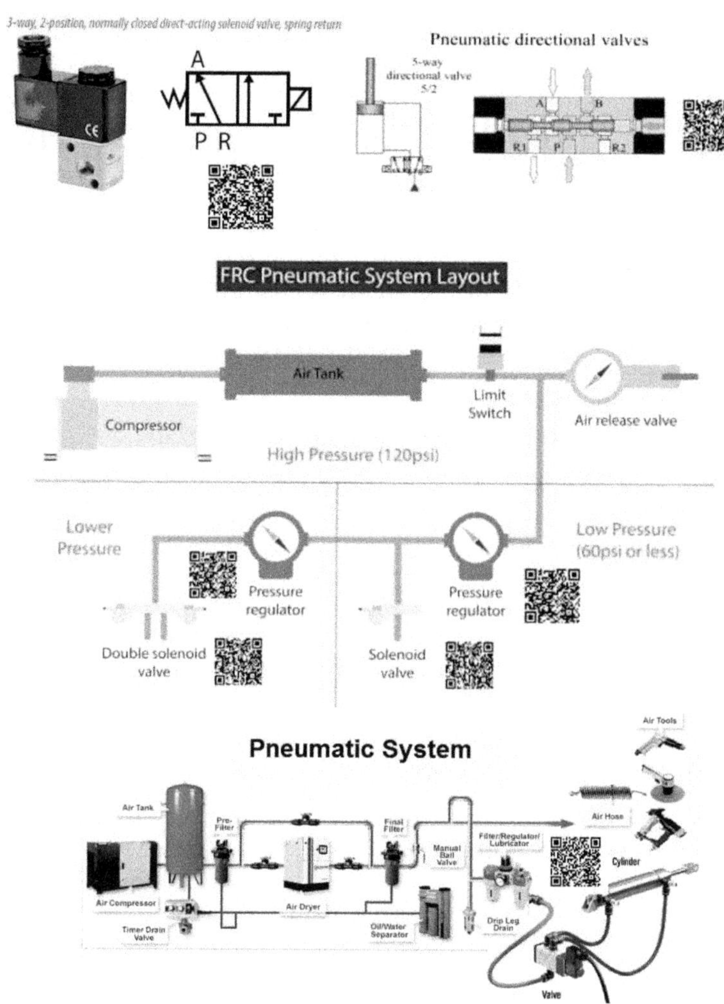

Enter Caption

CHAPTER FOUR

Structural Engineering MCQ

Safety Precaution in Structural Engineering

01] In case of bleeding, take treatment Of

A] spray cold water

B] Bandage immediately -----]

C] Enquire about the accident thought treatment

D] cold 3" and rest

02] in case of an accident, the victim should im

A] Asked to take rest

C] Attended immediately

D] leave him

03] First aid is given to an injured or ill person primarily....

A] Save life

B] Prevent further deterioration of the muff's

C] Give best possible comfort

D] All of these

04] Colour code for Bins for waste paper segregation is -----

A] blue Colour

B] Yellow Colour

C] Red Colour

D] Green Colour

05] In Japanese Seiko stands for -------------

A] Shine

B] Sort

C] Standardize

D] Sustain

06] Benefit of SS system is ------

A] Increase in productivity

B] Increase in quality

C] Reduction in wastage of time

D] All of these

07] Safety is -----------

A] nobody's business

B] every bodise business

C] Some bodies business

D] The organization business

08] For basic categories of safety signs are available The meaning of"prohibition" sign ----

A] shows it must not be done

B] Shows what must be done

C] Warns the hazard or danger

D] Gives information of safety provision

09] Which one is a workshop safety?

A] Keep shop floor clean and free from grease, oil or other slippery materials

B] Stop the machine before changing the speed

C] Don't use cracked or chipped tools

D] Don't try to stop a running machine with hand

10] In Personal Protect Equipment (PPE] HELMET is used to

A] protect head

B] Protect eyes

C] Protect hands

D] Protect ears

11] Which of the following belongs to general safety?

A Have a worker in good attitude

B] The work clean and clear

C] Concentrate on your work

D] Keep the floor and gangways clean and clear

12] While grinding, which is used to protect the eyes?

A] Dark green glass

B] Mask

C] Sun glasses

D] Safety goggles

13] Which of the following is done for machine safety?

A] Check the oil level before starting the machine

B] Do things in a methodical way

C] Keep the floor and gangways clean and clear

D] Don't use dies and scarves

14] In Personal Protect Equipment (PPE], 'sleeves' is used to protect ----------

A] Face

B] Eyes

C] Ears

D] Hands

15] ABC stands for --------------

A] Automatic Breathing Control

B] Automatic Blood Control

C] Airway Breathing Circulation

D] Automatic Blood Circulation

16] To put off"Class B" fire, the types of fire extinguisher used is ....]

A] dry power

B] Carbon dioxide

C] Jet of water

D] Foam type

17] Which type of fire extinguisher is used to put off general fire?

A] Water type Extinguisher

B] Foam type Extinguisher

C] Dry chemical powder Extinguisher

D] Carbon dioxide (C02] Extinguisher

Hand Tools in Structural Engineering

18] One micrometer (U] is equal to...

A] 0.1mm

B] 0.01mm

C] 0.001mm

D] 0.0001mm

19] Name the tool used to make and finish the leak proof joints of a pipe T joint

A] groover

B] setting hammer

C] creasing hammer

D] round bottom stake

20] Portion of the hammer used for fixing the handle is...

A] Face

B] Peen

C] Cheek

D] Eye hole

21] Weight of the hammer for the marking purpose is...

A] 250g

B] 500g

C] 1 kg

D] 2 kgs

22] To cut out small apertures which punch and die type of machine is used?

A] shear type nibbler

B] punch type nibbler

C] circular cutting machine

D] guillotine shearing machine

23] Scribers are made of...

A] Mild steel

B] High carbon steel

C] Brass

D] Cast iron

24] The size of an engineer's vice is specified by the...

A] Length of the movable jaw

B] Width of the jaws

C] Height of the vice

D] Maximum opening of the jaws

vice Bench vice

Bench Vice

25] The form of thread used in carpenters vice is...

A] Square

B] Acme thread

C] Sawtooth Thread

D] Knuckle thread

26] The convexity of files helps...

A] To file concave surfaces

B] To file convex surfaces

C] To prevent rounding of edges of work

D] The file to become straight when pressure is applied

27]] Name the instrument used to check the perpendicularity of the branch pipe with the main pipe of a pipe T joint

A] protractor

B] try square

C] spirit level

D] straight edge

28] The caliper meant for measuring the width of a slot is...

A] Odd leg caliper

B] Outside caliper

C] Jenny caliper

D] Inside calliper

29] The included angle of the groove of 'V' block is always....

A] 45°

B] 60°

C] 90°

D] 120°

v blocks

v block

'V' blocks

30] 'V' blocks are available in grades of...

A] A & B

B] A,B & C

C] 1,2 & 3

D] 1 & 2

31] 'V' blocks of grade 'B' are made of

A] Cast iron

B] Mild steel

C] Steel

D] Cast steel

32] 'V' block 50/5-40 A is used for holding jobs of diameter

A] Ø 50 mm

B] Ø 5 to Ø 50 mm

C] Ø 5 to Ø 40 mm

D] Ø 40 mm

33] The reason for using cast iron in making 'V' blocks

A] to increase the weight of the block

B] to reduce the cost
C] to reduce the friction
D] to get a good appearance

34] For cutting thin tubing, the most suitable pitch of the hacksaw blade is...
A] 1.8mm
B] 1.4mm
C] 1mm
D] 0.8mm

35] For cutting solid brass, the most suitable pitch of the hacksaw blade is...
A] 1.8mm
B] 1.4mm
C] 1mm
D] 0.8mm

36] A new hacksaw blade after a few strokes becomes loose because of the...
A] Stretching of the blade
B] Wing-nut threads being worn out
C] Wrong pitch of the blade
D] Improper selection of the set of saws.

37] While cutting small diameter pipes, it is advisable to watch regularly and ensure that...
A] The cut is along the curved line
B] More saw teeth are in contract
C] The work is not overheated
D] Proper balancing of hacksaw is maintained

Drilling in Structural Engineering

38] If the drill runs untrue, it will
A] get too hot
B] cut undersize
C] distort the spindle
D] cut an oversized hole

39] Running the drill too fast many result in
A] spoiling the cutting edge
B] poor surface finish
C] twisting the tang
D] drilling an oval hole

40] A drill with worn land will

A] drill hole oversize

B] <u>drill hole undersize</u>

C] run out of centre

D] drill an accurate hole

41] The morse taper provided on drills used on lathe ranges between

A] <u>MT1 to MT5</u>

B] MT1 to MT4

C] MT0 to MT5

D] MT0 to MT4

42] Feeding the small drill too fast into the work may result in

A] <u>breaking the drill</u>

B] bending the drill

C] cutting an oval shape hole

D] increased production

43] The drill size for a M 20 tap is

A] <u>17.5 mm</u>

B] 18 mm

C] 18.5 mm

D] 19 mm

44] The taper shank drills are held on the machine by means of...

A] Chucks

<u>B] Sleeves</u>

C] Drift

D] Vice

45] Drill chucks are fitted on the drilling machine spindle by means of a...

A] Knurled ring

<u>B] Arbor</u>

C] Drift

D] Pinion and key

drill chuck

drilling

Drill Chuck

46] The Morse taper provided on drills ranges between...

A] MT 1 to MT 5

B] MT 1 to MT 4

C] MT 0 to MT 5

D] MT 0 to MT 4

47] A drift is used for...

A] Drawing a drill location

B] Fixing chuck on the machine spindle

C] Removing a broken drill from the work

D] Removing the drill from the machine spindle

48] When the taper shank of the drill is larger than the machine spindle, the device to hold the drill is a...

A] Drill sleeve

B] Taper socket

C] Drill drift

D] Chuck and key

49] A special feature of the radial drilling machine is...

A] It can be used for drilling with a H.S.S] drill
B] Table can be moved and set at any position
C] A variety of speeds is available
D] The spindle can be brought to any position
50] The point angle of drills depends on...
A] The size of the drill
B] The type of machine
C] The material of the work
D] The RPM of the drill
51] The point angle for a standard drill is...
A] 60◦
B] 108◦
C] 118◦
D] 135◦
52] The helical angle determines the...
A] Cutting angle
B] Chew angle
C] Rake angle
D] Lip angle
53] The clearance angle of the drill is between...
A] 3◦ to 5◦
B] 8◦ to 12◦
C] 12◦ to 20◦
D] 15◦ to 20◦
54] The relief angle provided behind the cutting edge is called the..
A] Point angle
B] Chisel edge angle
C] Helix angle
D] Clearance angle
55] A set of number drill series consists of drills in the following ranges] Indicate the correct range
A] 1 to 40
B] 1 to 50
C] 1 to 80
D] 1 to 100
56] In the number drill series, the smallest drill size is...
A] 0.1 mm

B] 0.35 mm

C] 0.5 mm

D] 0.52 mm

57] In the number drill series, the largest drill size is...

A] 102 mm

B] 5.791 mm

C] 5.613 mm

D] 5.410 mm

58] In the letter drill series, the size of the drill 'A' is equal to ...

A] 13 mm

B] 6.08 mm

C] 6.045 mm

D] 5.944 mm

59] In the letter drill series, the largest drill size is equal to...

A] 10.33 mm

B] 10.490 mm

C] 12.01 mm

D] 15.00 mm

60] In a remote place (no electricity available] a rail track is to be drilled] Choose the right drilling machine

A] Radial drilling machine

B] Pillar drilling machine

C] Ratchet drilling machine

D] Sensitive drilling Machine

61] A drilling machine used by a carpenter for cabinet making is a...

A] Ratchet drilling machine

B] Radial drilling machine

C] Breast drilling machine

D] Sensitive drilling machine

62] Surface plates are made of...

A] High grade cast steel

B] Fine-grained cast iron

C] Alloy steels

D] Wrought iron

63] The drill size for a M 20 tap is

A] 17.5 mm

B] 18 mm

C] 18.5 mm

D] 19 mm

64] Tapping is mostly done to produce

A] external 'V' thread

B] <u>internal 'V' thread</u>

C] external square thread

D] internal square thread

65] The drill size for tapping is

A] more than the tap size

B] <u>less than the tap size</u>

C] equal to the tap size

D] either more or less than the tap size

66] which one of the following is the most suitable tap for lathe work?

A] spiral tap

B] <u>machine tap</u>

C] hand tap

D] left hand tap

67] A die is turned with a

A] die wrench

B] <u>diestock</u>

C] die plate

D] die handle

68] A tumbler gear unit has

A] a single gear

B] two gears

C] <u>three gears</u>

D] four gears

69] The cutting edge of a solid tool is made of

A] <u>carbon steel</u>

B] mild steel

C] super high speed steel

D] stelite

70] The tip of a cemented carbide threading tool is

A] <u>brazed</u>

B] welded

C] soldered

D] clamped to the shank

71] Tool will rub against the work surfaces and the cutting force increases when..

A] The clearance angle is more

B] The clearance angel is less

C] The rake angle is more

D] The rake angle is less

72] Formation of a chip while cutting is based on the...

A] Rake angle of the tool

B] Clearance angle of the tool

C] Wedge angle of the tool

D] Clearance and wedge angle of the tool

73] The suitable cutting fluid for drilling mild steel in a drilling machine is...

A] Synthetic soluble oil

B] Neat oil

C] Distilled water

D] Soluble oil

74] Centre drilling is an operation of...

A] Drilling and countersinking

B] Drilling and counter boring

C] Marking the centre location before drilling

D] Enlarging the diameter of a hole

75] Shaft ends are centre drilled for...

A] Supporting jobs between centres

B] Lubricating the dead centre

C] Reducing the weight

D] Assisting counter boring

76] The Centre drill size is selected on the basis of the

A] length of the job

B] material of the job

C] diameter of the job

D] type of operation

77] Centre drilling is done at a

A] high spindle speed with a high feed

B] low spindle speed with a high feed

C] high spindle speed with a low feed

D] low spindle speed with a low feed

Measuring Instruments in Structural Engineering

78] The least count of vernier caliper is

A] 0.01 mm

B] 0.02mm

C] 0.001 mm

D] 0.2 mm

vernier caliper

vernier caliper

Vernier Caliper

79] The graduations of a depth micrometer are...

A] Similar to an outside micrometer

B] In the reverse direction to that of the outside micrometer, both Thimble and sleeve

C] In the reverse direction only on the sleeve

D] In the direction only on the thimble

depth micrometer

depth micrometer

Depth Micrometer

80] The process of enlarging the end of a hole for accommodating the socket screw head is...

A] Reaming

B] Spot facing

C] Counter boring

D] Counter sinking

boring

Boring Operation

81]While choosing a boring tool for boring a given diameter, select

A] a long tool

B] a short tool

C] a long and stout tool

D] a short and stout tool

82] The cutting edge of the boring tool should be set for a small hole so that it is

A] 0.5 mm above the center

B] 0.5 mm below the center

C] 1 mm above the center

D] in the exact center

83] Bored holes are to be chamfered by using

A] a drill

B] triangular scraper

C] a cranked boring tool

D] a flat file

84] The tool used for boring deep holes is a

A] lathe mandrel

B] sleeve

C] drill

D] boring bar

E] auger bit

85] The cutting speed for rough boring is the

A] same as rough turning

B] same as drilling

C] same as knurling

D] same as thread cutting

86] The reamer is used for...

A] Drilling holes in thin sheets

B] Drilling deep holes

C] Removing burrs

D] Enlarging and finishing holes

reamer

reamer

Reamer

87] The reamer teeth are unevenly spaced because...

A] They are easy to manufacture

B] They can reduce chattering

C] They help to cut metal gradually

D] They help to remove the reamer easily

88] Which among the following is not a capability of reamers?

A] Finishing small holes

B] Finishing any machined profiles

C] Accuracy to closer limits

D] Producing high quality surface finish

89] The most important quality of any cutting fluid is

A] emulsification

B] specific heat

C] specific gravity

D] viscosity

Cutting Fluid

90] By using coolants on workpieces we can choose

A] higher cutting speeds

B] lower cutting feeds

C] lower cutting speeds

D] heavy depth of cuts

91] The cutting speed for aluminium with H.S.S] tools is

A] 30 m/min

B] 50 m/min

C] 70 m/min

D] 130 m/min

92] The cutting speed for brass with a H.S.S] tool is

A] 10 m/min

B] 25 m/min

C] 70 m/min

D] 140 m/min

93] The distance, which the cutting edge of a tool passes over the material in a minute while machining is Know as...

A] RPM

B] Feed

C] Machine speed

D] Cutting speed

94] The cutting angle for chipping cast iron is...

A] 37.5°

B] 55°

C] 60°

D] 90°

95] The depth of cut is given by

A] the top slide
B] the cross-slide
C] the compound slide
D] adjusting the tool
96] For mounting a lathe chuck
A] start it by hand and then turn the power on
B] mount it on by power
C] mount it by hand
D] mount it with the help of a hammer

lathe chucks

lathe chuck

Lathe Four Jaw Chuck

97] The morse taper provided on drills used on lathe ranges between
A] MT1 to MT5
B] MT1 to MT4
C] MT0 to MT5
D] MT0 to MT4
98] Feeding the small drill too fast into the work may result in
A] breaking the drill
B] bending the drill

C] cutting an oval shape hole

D] increased production

99] Number of flutes in a twist drills are --------

A] 1

B] 2

C] 3

D] 4

100] Which one of the following drilling machines is used for drilling holes where electricity is not available?

A] Bench drilling machine

B] Pillar drilling machine

C] Redial drilling machine

D] Ratchet drilling machine

101] Which one of the following drilling machine is used for heavy duty work?

A] Bench drilling machine

B] Pillar drilling machine

C] Radial drilling machine

D] Electric hand drilling machine

102] The suitable cutting fluid for drilling mild steel in a lathe is

A] synthetic soluble oil

B] neat cutting oil

C] distilled water

D] soluble oil+water

103] The suitable cutting fluid for precision grinding is

A] Soluble oil

B] Synthetic soluble oil

C] Neat oil

D] Servo Cut's'

gringing wheel grinding wheel

Grinding Wheel

104] Advantage of using cutting fluid during grinding operation is ------
A] 5000 surface finish
B] Reduction in cutting forces
C] Reduction in hardening of the work piece
D] All of these]
105] Lubricant is necessary to ....]
A] run the machine smoothly taking least load
B] Run the machine quickly
C] Stop the machine immediately
D] Produce work piece of greater accuracy
106] The main purpose for using a lubricant in machine tools is to ------
A] Cool down the making parts
B] Prevent machine tool from heating
C] Wet the making parts for close contact
D] Minimize the friction between the making parts
107] Driving plates are used for
A] mounting fixtures and workpieces
B] driving shafts between Centre's with a lathe dog
C] facing operations only
D] internal operations only
108] Balancing is done in the face plate work
A] to increase the speed
B] to reduce the pressure on the tool
C] for uniform rotation of work
D] to get a good finish
109] A face plate is used to hold
A] a round job
B] a finished job
C] an irregular Job
D] a hollow job
110] Which is correct angle plate used with face plate
(A] Solid Type
(B] Box Type
(C] Adjustable Type
(D] None of them

angle plate

Angle Plate

111] Face plate is made from.....]

(A] Mild Steel

(B] Cast Iron

(C] Brass

(D] Aluminium

112] Which following accessories is use for odd an uneven job turning?

(A] Three Jaw Chuck

(B] Two Jaw Chuck

(C] Driving Plate

(D] Face Plate

113] An irregular shaped work piece is turned on a Lathe] Which one of the following work holding accessories is used?

A] Two Jaw chuck

B] Three Jaw chuck

C] Driving plate

D] Face plate

114]The pads of a steady rest are made of

A] carbon steel

B] lead

C] mild steel

D] brass

steady rest

Steady Rest

115] A steady rest is used
A] to hold jobs
B] for face plate work
C] to drive the job
D] to support the job
116] A follower steady is held on the
A] lathe bed
B] lathe carriage
C] lathe spindle
D] tailstock
117] When turning long work pieces, the following is used
A sleeve
B change gear
C steady rest
D bracket]
118] Knurling operation is done at the
A] turning spindle speed
B] high spindle speed
C] 1/3 of the turning spindle speed
D] 1/2 of the turning spindle speed

knurling tool

Knurling Tool

119] Knurling is the operation of

A] shearing

B] forming

C] turning

D] pressing

120] Mandrels are generally used when machining with

A] heavy cuts

B] short facing cuts

C] light cuts

D] boring tools

Limit Fit & Tolerances in Structural Engineering

121] In the B.I.S system 25 hole deviations are specified by

A] small letters

B] small letters with numbers

C] small letters with tolerance

D] capital letters

122] The standard range of sizes covered in the B.I.S] system of limits and fits are

A] 0 to 10 mm

B] 0 to 100 mm

C] 25 to 400 mm

D] 0 to 500 mm

123] The basic size is the size

A] mentioned in the drawing

B] machined by the operator

C] based on which deviations are given

D] given by the instructor

124] Limits of size are

A] 2

B] 3

C] 4

D] 5

125] The number of fundamental deviations in the B.I.S] system are

A] 20

B] 22

C] 25

D] 28

126] The number of grade of tolerances in the B.I.S] system are

A] 12

B] 16

C] 18

D] 20

127] The size based on which the dimensional deviations are given is called...

A] Actual size

B] Basic size

C] Minimum limit of size

D] Maximum limit of Size

128] The size of parts made by .....] for provide interchange ability properties] (A] Measurement System

(B] Trial and Error System

(C] Limit and Tolerance System

(D] None of Them

129] Your job taper is correct if it is measured

A above the higher limit

B in between higher and lower limit

C below the lower limit]

130] When tolerance given in one side of the basic dimension, it is called --------

A].Tolerance system

B] Unilateral tolerance

C] Bilateral tolerance

D] Allowance System

131] A dimension is stated as (025 H7 in a drawing] The lower limit is -----------

A] 24.75 mm

B] 24.85 mm

C] 25.00 mm

D] 25-021 mm

132] The measured Size Of the dimensions of a component as called---------

A] Basic size

B] Nominal Size

C] Allowed size

D] Actual size

133] In the drawing the dimensions of a shaft is shown 40i 0068/0042, which is the size of Shaft within the tolerance?

A] 4.0.64 mm

B] 40.042 mm

C] 40.000 mm

D] 39.998 mm

134] In Hole basic system ----------

A] The size of the shaft is made constant

B] The Size of the hole is made constant

C] Only 'allowance is given on the hole

D] The permissible tolerance are given on the hole and the Shaft

135] The Size of a component is given as 24 -0.1] What does -O.1 indicates? _

A] Upper deviation is + 0.1 mm]

B] Lower deviation is 0.0 mm

C] Fundamental deviation is 0.0 mm

D] Lower deviation is _0.1 mm

136] The tolerance of a hole iS the difference between the -------

A] Maximum hole Size and maximum Shaft size

B] Maximum hole size and maximum hole Size

C] Minimum'hole size and maximum Shaft Size

D] Minimum hole Size and minimum shaft Size

137] A hole whose lower deviation is zero is called basic hole] Which one of the following letter indicates basic hole?]

A] E

B] F

C] G '

D] H

138] Which one having upper deviation zero?

A] Bassc Shaft

B] Basic hole

C] Tolerance

D] Clearance

139] A ball bearing on a shaft is type of fit? ,

A] Clearance fit

B] Driving fit

C] Shrinkage fit

D] None of the above

140] Which one of the following is important factor required to achieve the interchange ability in mass production?]

A] Geometrical accuracy]

B] Standardization

C] Dimensional accuracy

D] Surface finish

141] In the BIS system of limits and fits, the grade of tolerance are represented by number Symbols and there are ---------i

A] 14 grades of tolerance

B] 16 grades of tolerance

C] 18 grades of tolerance ‘

D] 20 grades of tolerance

142] A Product is said to have the quality when ....]

A] Its shape and dimensions are within the limit

B] It is fit for use

C] It appears to be very good

D] The choice of material is right

143] The maximum clearance required between hole’30 +0.021, 0.000 and shaft 30 -0.110, 0.143 is.

A] 0.110 mm ‘

B]0.131 mm

C] 0.164 mm

D] 0.143 mm

144] A dimension is stated as 25 .1002 mm in a drawing] What is the tolerance?

A] +0.02 mm’

B] +0.04 mm

C] -0.02 mm

D] 25.00 mm

145] A pin is fitted in a hole] The tolerance zone of the pin is entirely above that of hole] The fit obtained will be?

A] Clearance fit

B] Transition fit

C] Interference fit

D] Running fit

146] Interchange ability is normally applied for? _

A] Repairing of parts

B] Mass production

C] Single piece production

D] All of these

147] Tolerance is given to the part size to...........]

A] Production the part within the required permissible size error

B] Increase the production

C] Decrease the Production

D] Finish the components approximately

148] Which one of the following is the clearance fit under the whole basic system?

A] 20 H7/p6‘

B] 2067/211

C] ZOG/gll]

D] 20H/g11]

149] The three classes of fits as per BIS system aré ....] ~]

A] Clearance fit, interference fit and transition fit

B] Medium fit, push fit and tight fit

C] Flat fit, round fit and square fit

D] ‘Sliding fit ’, loose fit and shrinkage fit

150] Which one of the following tolerance specifications has a maximum dimensionless than 20 mm?

A] 20 +0.2,-0.3

B] 20 320.2

C] 20 -0.2, 0.3 e

D]m 20 +500, ~03

151] Difference between the maximum and minimum limit is -~-~~~~-~~~~~ ‘

A] Single informant

B] Basic shaft

C] Clearance

D] Tolerance

152] A shaft 55 running freely in bush bearing the type of fit is ---------

A] Clearance fit

B] Driving plate

C] shrinkage fit

D] None of the above

153] The taper ratio of the morse taper is

A] 1 in 10

B] 1 in 15

C] 1 in 20

D] 1 in 25

154] The morse standard taper is available in

A] 16 Nos

B] 12 Nos

C] 10 Nos

D] 8 Nos

155] Taper turning by offsetting the tailstock method can produce

A] an internal taper

B] an internal taper thread

C] an external taper

D] both external and internal tapers

taper turning

taper turning attachment

Taper by Tailstock Offset

156] By using the taper turning attachment, tapers can be turned with a setting angle up to

A] 10°

B] 15°

C] 20◦

D] 30◦

157] The accuracy of a taper is generally checked by means of......

A] taper gauges

B] gauge blocks

C] indicator and height gauge

D] 'V' blocks

158] Turning tapers by the compound rest method involves working solely with

Decimal measurements

B fractional measurements

C metric measurements

D angular measurements]

159] Long tapers are produced

A with the taper turning attachment

B with the compound slide

C by setting over the tail stock

D by adjusting the cross slide]

160] The length of turned tapers are checked with

A vernier calliper

B micrometer

C inside callper

D dial test indicator]

161] The disadvantages of taper turning using the com] pound slide are

A] only long tapers can be turned

B] only very large tapers can be turned

C] only manual in feed is possible

D] only short tapers can be turned due to the restrictions of the compound slide]

162] External tapers are checked with

A] limit plug gauge

B] taper ring gauge

C]taper plug gauge

D] thread plug gauge]

163] The use of a taper turned on lathe is ----

A] Assist to transmit drive in the assembled parts

B] Used for Assembly and disassembly of parts

C] Give self alignment in the assembled parts

164] Which type of method is used in mass production of production of producing small length of taper?

A] Form tool

B] Compound slide

C] Tailstock offset.

D] Taper turning attachment

165] Morse standard taper is one of the internationally accepted standards taper, which is available in numbers from--------

A]1to7

B]1 to 8

C] O to 7

D] 0 to 8

166] Which taper turning method is used for cutting steep taper?

A] Set over method

B] Taper turning attachment

C] Form tool

D] Swivelling the compound rest

167] Morse taper is used in which of the following machine components -...

A] Spindles of lathe

B] Spindles of drill machine

C] Shanks of reamers

D] All of these

168] For mass production of the taper which one of the following method is used.......]

A] Tailstock offset method

B] Taper turning attachment method

C] Form too method

D] Compound slide method

169] The major diameter of the taper is 40 mm, minor diameter is 30 mm] The total length of the job is 100 mm is tapered then offset is given by -

A] 5 mm

B] 7.5 mm

C] 12 mm

D] 9 mm

170] The accuracy of an ordinary bevel protractor is --' ------------degree]

A] One

B] Three

C] Two

D] Four

171] The least count of a vernier bevel protractor is...

A] 1"

B] 5'

C] 1◦

D] 5 ◦

172] The part of a vernier bevel protractor which is normally used as a reference base for measuring angles is the...

A] Blade

B] Stock

C] Disc

C] Main scale

173] The part of a vernier bevel protector on which main scale divisions are marked is the...

A] Stock

B] Dial

C] Disc

D] Adjustable blade

174] The part of a bevel protractor, which comes in contact with the inclined surface while measuring is the...

A] Blade

B] Stock

C] Disc

D] Dial

175] The value of each division of the main scale of a vernier bevel protractor is...

A] 5'

B] 1◦

C] 5◦

D.10◦

176] The value of each division of the vernier scale of a bevel protractor is...

A] 1◦

B] 1◦5'

C] 1◦55'

D.5'

177] The part of the vernier bevel protractor on which main scale divisions are marked

A stock

B dial

C disc

D adjustable blade

178] In Vernier bevel protractor is designed to measure?

A] Acute angles

B] Obtuse angles

C] Acute and Obtuse angle

D] Liner dimensions

179] To get least count of 5 in a vernier bevel protractor the 23° main scale are divided into -..

A] 12 equal parts on vernier scale

B] 22 equal parts on vernier scale

C] 24 equal parts on vernier scale

D] 25 equal parts on vernier scale

180] Which of the following is not the part of a combination set?

A] Stock

B] Square head

C] Protractor head

D] Centre head

181] The datum, form which the measurements of the vernier height gauge are taken, is...

A] The beam

B] The vernier slide

C] The base

D] Above the scriber poing

vernier height gauge vernier height guage

Vernier Height Gauge

182]The part of a vernier height gauge on which the main scale divisions are graduated is the...

A] Base

B] Beam

C] Fine setting device

D] The vernier plate

183] On which part of the vernier height gauge are the main scale division graduated?]

A] Base

B] Vernier plate

C] Beam

D] Fine adjusting unit

184] For marking purpose a Vernier height gauge must be on the --------

A] Bed of a machine tool

B] Surface plate

C] Square block

D] Any flat surface

185] Before using Vernier height gauge make sure that the --------

A] Locking screw is in a locked position

B] Scriber is Locked

C] Zero of the vernier coincides with zero of the main scale

D] Gib is Provided

186] The least count Of a vernier height gauge is...........]

A] 0.05 mm

B] 0.1 mm

C] 0.02 mm

D] 0001 mm

187] Which laying out the vernier height gauge must be used on the ----------

A] V block

B] Machine bed

<u>C] Surface plate</u>

D] Any flat surface

188] The part which is slides on the beam of a vernier height gauge is known as a ------

A] Base

B] Beam scale

C] Scriber

<u>D] Vernier slide</u>

189] The base of the vernier height gauge is generally made out of ---------

A] Cast iron]

<u>B] Steel</u>

C] Aluminium alloy

D] Tungsten carbide

190] Which instrument iis used for marking layout?

A] Micrometer

B] Vernier

C] Depth gauge

<u>D] Vernier height gauge</u>

191] While marking with a Vernier height gauge, the work piece is generally ----------

<u>A] Supported by an angle plate</u>

B] Supported by another work piece

C] Held by one hand

D] Held without support

192] Which of the following is not the part of a combination set?

<u>A] Stock</u>

B] Square head

C] Protractor head

D] Centre head

Engineering Drawing in Structural Engineering

18]The 'T' square is used for drawing lines ......

a] inclined

b] curved

c] vertical

d] horizontal

19] For drawing large size circle is drawn by.....

a] straight bar

b] lengthening bar

c] big bar

d] small bar

20] To draw or measure angle is used by.....

a]set square

b] protractor

c] 'T' square

d] none of these

21] The grade of pencil is used to sketching lettering ....

a] conical point

b] chisel point

c] soft

d] low

22] For drawing thin lines of uniform thickness the pencil should be sharpened in the form of ....

a] chisel edge

b]conical

c] pointed

d] none of these

23] What is used for drawing curves which can not drawn by compass

a] small compass

b] French curve

c] protractor

d] none of these

24]Unnecessary lines is removed by .....

a] Duster

b] sand paper block

c] eraser

d] none of these

25] Circle and arcs are drawn by means of .....l.

a] compass

b] divider

c] lengthening bar

d]none of these

26] Inking pen is used in drawing ......

a] horizontal line

b] non circular arcs

c] vertical lines

d] all of these

27] The card board scale are available in set of .....

a] 7

b] 8

c] 6

d] 9

28] The convenient length size of 30 -60°-90° set square for used in school and colleges are......

a] 250

b] 200

c] 300

d] none of these

29] Drawing board is shape of ....

a] square

b] rectangular

c] triangular

d] none of these

30] The 'T' square , set square ,scale protractor are complain use in.......

a] protractor

b] mini drafter

c] set square

d] none of these

31]Set square , T square edges are bevelled for the purpose of....

a] curve line

b] inking lines

b] taking measurements

d] none of these

32]Geometrical construction which are mostly based on plane geometry and which are very.......

a] Accuracy

b] Quality

c] Essential

d] Superior quality

33] How much method of drawing the regular polygons.......

a] Inscribe circle method and arc method

b] General method for drawing any polygon

c] Alternative method

d] All of these

34] The line AB can be divided into .... equal parts.

a] 7

b] 10

c] 15

d] All of them

35] Which method of constructing triangl in circle......

a] Inscribing

b] Describing

c] Both a and b

d] None of these

36] When two sides of the hexagon are required to be horizontal the starting point for stepping equal division should be on an end of the.....

a] Horizontal diameter

b] Vertical diameter

c] Inclined diameter

d] None of these

37] If two sides of hexagon are required to be vertical the starting point should be on an end of the....

a] Inclined diameter

b] Horizontal diameter

c] Vertical diameter

d] None of these

38] The section obtained by the inter section of the right circular cone by a plane in different position relative to the axis of the cone are called.......

a] Conics

b] Circles

c] Triangles

d] Half circle

39] When the section plane is inclined to the axis and cuts all the generators on one side on a apex the section is in......

a] Conic section

b] Ellipse

c] Parabola

d] Hyperbola

40] When the section plane is inclined to the axis and is parallel to one of the generators the section is a ....

a] Ellipse
b] Parabola
c] Hyperbola
d] Cycloid

41] Use of elliptical curve is........

a] Arches
b] Dams and monuments
c] Manholes, gland & stuffing boxes
d] All of these

42] Use of parabolic curve is.........

a] Bridges & arches
b] Sound reflectors
c] Light reflectors
d] All of these

43] Use of hyperbolical curve is......

a] Cooling towers and water channel
b] Dames
c] Bridges
d] All of these

44] When the point is within the circle, the curve is called an.......

a] Superior trochoid
b] Interior trochoid
c] Trochoid
d] Isotrochoid

45] When the point outside the circle then the curve is called as......

a] Interior trochoid
b] Superior trochoid
c] Trochoid
d] Insuperior trochoid

46] The curve general by a point on a circumference of a circle, which rolls without slipping along another circle it is called.......

a] Epicycloids
b] Hypocycloid
c] Involute
d] None of these

47] When the circle rolls inside another circle the curve is called.......

a] Hypocycloid
b] Epicycloids
c] Trochoid
d] <u>Hypotrochoid</u>
48] The use of archemedian spiral curve is made in........
a] Teeth profiles of helical gears
b] Profiles of cams
c] <u>Both a & b</u>
d] None of these
49] The cams are widely used in........
a] Automates
b] Printing machines
c] C engines
d] <u>All of these</u>
50] Spring index =
a] Diameter of coil / diameter of a wire
b] <u>Diameter of wire /diameter of coil</u>
c] Mean diameter of wire / diameter of coil
d] Mean diameter of a coil / diameter of wire
51] Eccentricity =
a] <u>Distance of a point from the focus / distance of the point from directrix</u>
b] Distance of focus from point / distance of point from
c] Distance of point from focus / distance of directrix of point
d] Distance of point from directrix / distance of point from focus
52] Mathematically an ellipse can be described by equation.....
a] $a^2 / X^2 + y^2 / b^2 = 1$
b] $x^2 / a^2 + y^2 / b^2$
c] $x^2 / a^2 + y^2 / b^2 = 0$
d] <u>$x^2 / a^2 + y^2 / b^2 = 1$</u>
53] Mathematically a parabola can be described by an equation......
a] $y^2 = 4ax$
b] $x^2 = 2ay$
c] $x^2 = 4ay$
d] <u>Both a & b</u>
54] Mathematically hyperbola can be described by an equation.......
a] <u>$x^2 /a^2 - y^2 /b^2 = 1$</u>
b] $x^2 /y^2 - y^2 /x^2 = 0$

c] Both a & b

d] None of these

55] Cycloid can be described by an equation......

a] y = a(1-cos Ø]

b] x = a(Ø -sin Ø]

c] Both a & b

d] None of these

56] The mathematically represented hypocycloid is.....

a] Y = a $\cos^3$ Ø, X = a $\sin^3$ Ø

b] X = a $\sin^3$ Ø, Y = a $\cos^3$ Ø

c] X = a $\cos^3$ Ø, Y = a $\sin^3$ Ø

d] None of these

57] Mathematically represented by involute is

a] X = r sin Ø - r Ø cos Ø, Y = r cos + r Ø sin Ø

b] X = r sin Ø + r cos Ø, Y = r cos Ø – r Ø sin Ø

c] Y = r Ø cos Ø – r sin Ø, X = r sin Ø – r Ø cos Ø

d] X = r cos Ø + r Ø sin Ø, Y =r sin Ø - r Ø cos Ø

58] The lines from the object to the plane are called.......

a] Projection

b] Projector

c] Reference plane

d] None of these

59] The orthographic projection an object is represented by View on the mutual perpendicular projection lines

a] Two or three

b] Three or two

c] Three or four

d] None of these

60] When the projectors are parallel to each other & also perpendicular to the plane, the projection is called......

a] Isometric projection

b] Oblique projection

c] Orthographic projection

d] Perspective projection

61] The two planes employed for the purpose of Orthographic projections are......

a] Auxillary plane

d] Horizontal plane

c] Reference plane

d] None of these

62] The line in which they intersect is termed the reference line & is denoted by the letters.......

a] AB

b] YZ

c] XY

d] None of these

63] The projection on the VP is called........

a] Side view

b] Front view

c] Top view

d] All of these

64] ....Method, when the views are drawn in their relative positions, the plane comes below the elevation. The view of the object as observed from the left-side the right of elevation.

a] Plane of projection

b] First angle projection

c] Third angle projection

d] None of these

65] Third angle projection method, the object is assumed to be situated in the........ quadrant.

a] First quadrant

b] Second quadrant

c] Third quadrant

d] Fourth quadrant

66] .... Method of projection is used in U.S.A & also in other countries.

a] plane of projection

b] Orthographic projection

c] First-angle projection

d] Third angle projection

67] When an object is situated on the ground, in first angle projection method, the bottom of its ..... will co-inside with XY

a] Top view

b] Front view

c] side view

d] All of these

68] The important element of this projection system

a] An object

b] Plane of projection

c] An observer

d] All of these

69] When line AB is parallel to HP hence ....

a] It' front view to AB

b] It''s side view equal to AB

c] It's top view equal to AB

d] None of these

70] When a line is parallel to a plane; it's projection on plane is equal to it's ;

a] True length

b] True shape

c] True size

d] None of these

71] The point is parallel in which the line or line produced meet the point is plane is called it's ....

a] Line

b] ratio

c] Trace

d] none of these

72] .... is the shortest distance between two points.

a] a line

b] a point

c] a straight line

d] none of these

73] When the line intersect horizontal plane that's called.....

a] horizontal trace

b] vertical trace

c] trace of line

d] none of these

74]Planes may be divided into two main types ......

a] Perpendicular planes, auxillary planes

b] Perpendicular plane, oblique planes

c] Auxillary planes , perpendicular planes

d] none of these

75] Planes which are inclined to the reference plane are called......

a] Auxillary plane

b] obliqeu plane

c] Perpendicular planes

d] picture plane

76] When a plane is perpendicular to a reference plane it's projection on that plane is a..........

a] horizontal line

b] parallel line

c] straight line

d] none of these

77] When a plane is parallel to a reference plane , it's projection on that plane shows........

a] It's true shape &size

b] It's true length & size

c] It's true height & size

d] none of these

78] Plane perpendicular to VP & HP that plane is called as ....

a] Auxillary Plane

b] Oblique Plane

c] Perpendicular Plane

d] None of these

79] Perpendicular plane can be divides into the following types.........

a] Perpendicular to both the reference planes.

b] Perpendicular to one plane & parallel to other

c] Perpendicular to one plane & inclined to other

d] All of these

80] The planes have only two dimensions, viz........

a] Length & breadth

b] Length & height

c] Length & thickness

d] All of these

81] The imaginary line of prism joining the centrs of the bases called.........

a] Faces

b] Axis

c] Apex

d] Base

82] A right & regular prism has it's axis....... to the bases

a] Parallel
b] Perpendicular
c] Inclined
d] None of these

83] When a pyramid or a cone is cut by a plane parallel to it's base thus removing the top portion, the remaining portion is called it's.........

a] Sphere
b] Cone
c] Cylinder
d] Frustum

84] Oblique cylinder & cones have their axes........ to their base

a] Inclined
b] Parallel
c] Perpendicular
d] All of these

85] Projection of two equal sphere s resting on the ground & in contact with each other, with the line joining there centre parallel to the..........

a] A VP
b] VP
c] HP
d] All of these

86] Projections of section on the other plane to which it is inclined is called.......

a] Section planes
b] Apparent section
c] True shape of sphere
d] None of these

87] When the section plane is parallel to the HP or the ground, the true shape of the section will be seen in.........

a] Front view
b] Side view
c] Top view
d] All of these

88] Surface of solid are laid out on a plane the figure obtained is called its........

a] Interpenetration
b] Development
c] Intersection

d] None of these

89] Development of surfaces is essential in.........

a] Foundry shop

b] Sheet metal work

c] Fitting shop

d] None of these

90] Which method of development used in transition pieces?

a] Parallel diameter

b] Radial line method

c] Triangulation method

d] Approximate method

91] Which method of development used in pyramids and cones.........

a] Radial line method

b] Parallel line method

c] Approximate method

d] Triangulation method

92] Parallel line method is used in..........

a] Prism

b] Cylinder

c] Cubes

d] All of these

93] Which method of development used in surface as sphere, paraboloid, ellipsoid, hyperboloid, and helicoids

a] Radial line method

b] Triangulation method

c] Approximate method

d] Parallel line method

94] Zone method and lune method is used in development of........

a] Prisms

b] Cones

c] Sphere

d] Pyramids

95] Calculation the subtended angle Θ by the formula $\Theta = 360^{0} \times$ radius of the base circle

a] Length of axis

b] Slant height

c] Radius of axis

d] None of these

96] In engineering practice, objects constructed may have constituent part, the surfaces of which intersect one another in lines called........ of intersection.

a] Lines

b] Cones

c] Cylinder

d] Prisms

97] The line of interaction may be depending upon the nature of.......

a] Intersection surface

b] Intersecting solids

c] Intersection cones

d] None of these

98] The two plane surface intersect in a........ line

a] Curve

b] Straight

c] Plane

d] All of these

99] The line of intersection between two curved surface or between......... Surface and a curved surface is a curve.

a] A curved

b] A plane

c] A solids

d] None of these

100] When a solids completely penetration another solids there will be two lines of intersection. These lines are sometimes called the line or........

a] Line of interpenetration

b] Curve of interpenetration

c] Solids of interpenetration

d] All of these

101] Use of penetration curve is.......

a] Sheet metal work

b] Fitting shop

c] Fabricating work

d] Foundry shop

102] Methods of determining the line of intersection between surface of two interpenetration.........

a] Approximate method & radial line method

b] Line method and cutting plane method

c] Triangulation method and parallel line method

d] None of these

103] Example of interpenetration is..........

a] Two prism intersection

b] Cylinder and prism intersection

c] Cone and cylinders intersection

d] All of these

104] Two cylinder intersection is example of.........

a] Intersection

b] Interpenetration

c] Cone intersection

d] None of these

105] .... Method is explained in detail while solving illustrative problems

a] Line method

b] Radial line method

c] Cutting plane method

d] Parallel line method

106] What is a type of isometric projection?

a] Pictorial projection

b] Orthographic projection

c] Perspective projection

d] Oblique Projection

107] Isometric views have been drawn........

a] Full scale

b] Half scale

c] True length

d] True scale

108] The line parallel to isometric axis are called........

a] Isometric axis

b] Isometric line

c] Isometric planes

d] Isometric views

109] The isometric projection is reduce in the ratio.........

a] 3 :

b] 1 : 2

c] 2 : 2

d] 2 : 3

110] The isometric projection of circle drawn with........

a] Isometric Plane

b] Isometric graph

c] Isometric Drawing

d] Isometric Scale

111] The major axis of the ellipse is long than...............

a] Radius of the circle

b] True diameter

c] Diameter of the circle

d] None of these

112] Makes practice for drawing of isometric view using........

a] Isometric planes

b] Isometric lines

c] Isometric graph

d] Isometric view

113] Use of parabolic curve is

a] Sound reflectors

b] Dams

c] Man hole of boiler

d] Gland & stuffing box

114] When the section plane is inclined the true shape of section on

a] AVP

b] VP

c] HP

d] A/P

115] When section plane is perpendicular to both the HP & VP the true shape of section on

a]Top view

b] Side view

c] Front view

d]None of this

116] When view projected on auxiliary planes are called

a] Auxiliary view

b Sectional view

c] Front view

d] None of these

117] Invisible features of an object are shown by means of

a] Outline

b] Chain lines

c] Hidden lines

d] None of these

118] Importance of sectional view on drawing for

a] Internal details

b] Outer details

c] Hatching

d] None of these

119] The component is cut by a straight cutting plane is divided in to two parts

a] Half section

b] Full section

c] Offset section

d] Removed section

120] section line is two different parts (pieces] in contact should be drown in...

a] Same direction

b] Opposite direction

c]parallel direction

d] None of these

121] When area to be sectioned in very small as for this plate and structural members blacked in section may be used. A space of not less than

a] 0.07mm

b] 0.7mm

c] 0.05mm

d] 0.5mm

122] The sum of interior angles of polygon is equal

a] (2*n-4]*Right angle

b] (2*n]*Right angle-4

c] (2*4-n]*Right angle

d] (2-4*n]*Right angle

123] One micron is equal to ....mm

a] 0.001

b] 1000

c] 0.01

d] 0.1

124] Development of surface is essential in.....

a] foundry shop

b] sheet metal work
c] fitting shop
d] none of these
125] Which method of development used in transition piece?
a] parallel line method
b] radial line method
c] triangulation method
d] none of these
126] The isometric projection is reduced in the ratio of
a] √2:√3
b] √3:√2
c] 1:√2
d] none of these
127] When measurements are required in three units the scale is used....
a] full scale
b] plain scale
c] half scale
d] none of these
128]Isometric drawing is larger in production about isometric projection is....
a] 22.5%
b] 0.815
c] 9/11
d] none of these
129] While isometric of sphere of spherical parts.......is must be used.
a] full scale
b] isometric length
c] true length
d] half scale
130] When circle draw with isometric scale the length of major axis of the ellipse to the ....
a] true diameter
b] isometric diameter
c] isometric diameter
d] none of these
131] In isometric view which contain a large number of non –isometric lines which method is used
a] box method

b] off-set method

c] co-ordinate method

d] centre lay out method

132] When drawing is drawn smaller than actual size of object .....

a] full scale

b] enlarging scale

c] reducing scale

d] none of these

133] When e=1 curve is called.....

a] parabola

b] hyperbola

c] ellipse

d] none of these

134]Compare with isometric drawing the advantage of oblique projection is....

a] front face is in true shape

b] two axis are always perpendicular to each othe

c] receding axis is taken at some convenient angles

d] none of these

135]If all the receding edges are drawn true length the oblique projection is called...

a] cavilier projection

b] cabinet projection

c] general projection

d] none of these

136] The large object such as building the point is usually taken height of .....

a] 0.8mm

b] 1.2mm

c] 1.8mm

d] 1.5mm

137] Central plane is the imaginary vertical plane which passes through....

a] P. P

b] H.L

c] G.P

d] C.P

138] When object is parallel to P.P the perspective is called......

a] one point
b] two point
c] three point
d] none of these

139] The line drawn through the station point from the picture plane shall be ....
a] P.A
b] H.L
c] G.L
d] C

140] The distance of the station point from the picture plane shall be .....
a] Max. Diameter of the object
b] Twice the max. Diameter of the object
c] Half the max. Diameter of the object
d] none of these

141] In isometric view of hexagonal plane all the sides of hexagon is .....
a] equal length
b] unequal length
c] none of these

142] When all the faces are equal & regular the polyhedron is said....
a] regular
b] prisms
c] irregular
d] pyramid

143] Oblique prisms &pyramid have ......
a] axis perpendicular to the base
b] axis inclined to the base
c] faces inclined to the H.P
d] none of these

144] Icosahedrons has equal equilateral triangular faces
a] 12
b] 8
c] 20
d] 6

145] When a pyramid or cone is cut by a plane parallel to its base is called.....
a] pyramid
b] turned carted

c] frustum

d] none of these

146] Plane which are inclined to both the reference plane is called ......

a] oblique plane

b] perpendicular plane

c] inclined plane

d] none of these

147] When a line parallel to H.P & perpendicular to V.P the trace line is.....

a] V.T

b] H.T

c] no trace

d] V.T& H.T

148] When a line parallel to the V.P and inclined to H.P the true length of line in.....

a] front view

b] top view

c] side view

d] none of these

149] When point situated in front quadrant

a] above the H.P & in front of V.P

b] below the H.P & in front of V.P

c] behind the V.P & above H.P

d] below the H.P & behind the V.P

150] Find the quadrant of point "b" is 15 mm above H.P and 25mm behind the V.P

a] I st

b] III rd

c] IIII th

d] II nd

151] In first angle projection front view is ......

a] above the top view

b] below the top view

c] above the side view

d] below the side view

152] In orthographic projection the projectors are ....

a] parallel to plane

b] perpendicular to plane

c] inclined to plane
d] none of these
153] L.H.S.V means.........
a] length of side view
b] left hand view
c] right hand view
d] left hand side view
154] The object lines between the observer and the plane of projection is ....
a] 3rd angle
b] 1st angle
c] 4th angle
d] 2nd angle
155] In third angle projection plane of projection is assumed to be ......
a] non transparent
b] quadrant
c] transparent
d] dihedral angle
156] In third angle projection top view is always on......
a] above front view
b] above top view
c] below the front view
d] below the side view
157] Four quadrants which may be called as......
a] anticlockwise
b] first and third angle
c] dihedral angles
d] none of these
158] In first angle projection method the view see from the left is placed on .....
a] left of the front view
b] right of front view
c] above the top view
d] below the front view
159] The size of A2 paper is .....
a] 297*420
b] 594*841
c] 420*594

d] 210*297

160] The edge of board on which 'T' square is sli9ding is called ......

a] straight edge

b] <u>working edge</u>

c] chisel edge

d] none of these

161] The size of title block as recommended by B.I.S . is .....

a] <u>185*65</u>

b] 150*50

c] 170*65

d] none of these

162] For A2 size sheet the number of zones suggested by B.I.S. along the length & width.......

a] 12,8

b] 16,12

c] 8,6

d] none of these

163] The drawing sheet is so folded that...... is always on the top.

a] drawing

b] lettering

c] title block

d] none of these

164] In free hand sketching horizontal lines are sketched from.......

a] right to left

b] up to down

c] left to right

d] none of these

165] When drawing is down smaller than actual size of object

a] enlarging scale

b] reducing scale

c] full scale

d] none of these

166] The ratio of the length of the object represented on drawing to the actual length of object is called.......

a] full scale

b] R.F.

c] half scale

d] plain scale

167] When measurements are required in three unit the scale is used.....
a] full scale
b] half scale
c] plain scale
d] none of these
168] When protractor is not available the scale of chord is used ......
a] measure length
b] measure angle
c] measure scale
d] none of these
169] The least count of a vernier calliper is ....
a] 0.001
b] 0.02
c] 0.001
d] 0.0002
170] Which scale is used to read a very small unit with great accuracy?
a] plain scale
b] diagonal scale
c] scale of chord
d] vernier scale
171] The R.F. is greater than one (1] the scale is ....
a] plain scale
b] diagonal scale
c] enlarging scale
d] reducing scale

Civil Engineering Fundamentals for Structural Engineering

1. Stones are obtained from rocks that are made up of:
a) Ores
b) Minerals
c) Chemical compounds
d) Crystals
2. Which one of the following is not a classification of stones?
a) Physical Classification
b) Mineralogical Classification
c) Chemical Classification
d) Practical Classification
3. The hot molten material occurring naturally below the surface of the Earth is called:

a) Lava
b) Slag
c) Magma
d) Tuff

4. At what depth and rate is a hypabyssal rock formed?
a) Slow cooling of magma at considerable depth
b) Quick cooling of magma at a shallow depth
c) Rapid cooling of magma at Earth's surface
d) Rapid cooling of magma at a shallow depth

5. What is a sedimentary deposit?
a) Weathered product remains at site
b) Weathered product carried away in solution
c) Weathered product gets carried away agents
d) Insoluble weathered product is carried away in suspension

6. Which factor disturbs the equilibrium of rocks, commencing metamorphism?
a) Increase in temperature
b) Decrease in temperature and pressure
c) Increase in temperature and pressure
d) Decrease in pressure

7. Which of the following is not a metamorphic change?
a) Calcite to schist
b) Limestone to marble
c) Shale to slate
d) Granite to gneisses

8. Which of the following rocks are hard and durable?
a) Argillaceous rocks
b) Siliceous rocks
c) Calcareous rocks
d) Carbonaceous rocks

9. Foliated structure is very common in case of:
a) Sedimentary rocks
b) Plutonic rocks
c) Igneous rocks
d) Metamorphic rocks

10. Granite is a type of:
a) Plutonic rock
b) Metamorphic rock

c) Hypabyssal rock
d) Volcanic rock

11. Which of the following is a good fire-resistant stone?
a) Clay
b) Granite
c) Quartz
d) Limestone

12. What is a freestone?
a) Stone free from impurities
b) Stone that doesn't require dressing
c) Metamorphic stone
d) Stone free from veins and planes of cleavage

13. Why are stones with lighter shades of colour preferred?
a) Easy to clean
b) Easily available
c) Don't spoil the appearance
d) Darker shades are heavier

14. Hardness is an important parameter considered in the construction of:
a) Slabs
b) Walls
c) Bridges
d) Arches

15. What is the required specific gravity for a good building stone?
a) Greater than 2.7
b) Less than 3
c) Greater than 3
d) Less than 2.7

16. The percentage absorption by weight of a good stone, after how many hours should not exceed .6?
a) 6 hrs
b) 12 hrs
c) 48 hrs
d) 24 hrs

17. What texture should a building stone possess?
a) Loose grains
b) Crystalline structure
c) Cavities

d) Cracks

18. Toughness index of a good stone should be more than:

a) 17

b) 18

c) 13

d) 19

Structural MCQ for Structural Engineering

1. Which of the following structural loads are not applied commonly to a building?

a) Dead load

b) Rain load

c) Live load

d) Environmental load

2. Dead load comprises of:-

a) Permanently attached loads

b) Temporarily attached loads

c) Permanent as well as temporary loads

d) Snow load

3. Live loads, with time can vary in:-

a) Magnitude

b) Position

c) Neither position nor magnitude

d) Position as well as magnitude

4. Most of the loads applied to a building are environmental load.

State whether this statement is true or false.

a) True

b) False

5. Building codes require the partition load to be considered even without partition if live load is less than:-

a) 60 psf

b) 70 psf

c) 80 psf

d) 90 psf

6. In the method used to establish the magnitude of live load, what is the reference time period?

a) 30 years

b) 35 years

c) 50 years

d) 60 years

7. Impact loads are equal to the sum of the magnitude of the loads actually caused and the magnitude if the loads had they been dead loads.

State whether this statement is true or false.

a) True

b) False

8. Impact load results from which type of effects of loads applied?

a) Static

b) Dynamic

c) Static and dynamic

d) Neither static nor dynamic

9. How does an increase in the pitch of the roof affects the amount of load that can be placed on it?

a) It increases

b) It decreases

c) Remains constant

d) Depends upon case

10. If R1 = 1.1 and R2 = 1.2, then what is value of Lr(in psf)?

a) 26.1

b) 26.2

c) 26.3

d) 26.4

Fluid Mechanics MCQ for Structural Engineering

1. Which one is in a state of failure?

a) Solid

b) Liquid

c) Gas

d) Fluid

2. A small shear force is applied on an element and then removed. If the element regains it's original position, what kind of an element can it be?

a) Solid

b) Liquid

c) Fluid

d) Gaseous

3. In which type of matter, one won't find a free surface?

a) Solid

b) Liquid

c) Gas

d) Fluid

4. If a person studies about a fluid which is at rest, what will you call his domain of study?

a) Fluid Mechanics

b) Fluid Statics

c) Fluid Kinematics

d) Fluid Dynamics

5. The value of the compressibility of an ideal fluid is

a) zero

b) unity

c) infinity

d) more than that of a real fluid

6. The value of the Bulk Modulus of an ideal fluid is

a) zero

b) unity

c) infinity

d) less than that of a real fluid

7. The value of the viscosity of an ideal fluid is

a) zero

b) unity

c) infinity

d) more than that of a real fluid

8. The value of the surface tension of an ideal fluid is

a) zero

b) unity

c) infinity

d) more than that of a real fluid

9. Which of the following statement is true about vapor pressure of a liquid?

a) Vapor pressure is closely related to molecular activity and temperature of the liquid

b) Vapor pressure is closely related to molecular activity but independent of the temperature of the liquid

c) Vapor pressure is not affected by molecular activity and temperature of the liquid

d) Vapor pressure is not affected by molecular activity and is independent of the temperature of the liquid

10. Which of the following equation correctly depicts the relation between the vapor pressure of a liquid and it's temperature?

a) Vapor pressure increases linearly with the increase in temperature of the liquid

b) Vapor pressure increases slightly with the increase in temperature of the liquid at low temperatures and the rate of increase goes high at higher temperatures

c) Vapor pressure increases rapidly with the increase in temperature of the liquid at low temperatures and the rate of increase goes low at higher temperatures

d) Vapor pressure remains unchanged with the increase in temperature of the liquid

11. Which of the following is the condition for the boiling of a liquid?

a) Absolute pressure of a liquid must be greater than or equal to it's vapor pressure

b) Absolute pressure of a liquid must be less than or equal to it's vapor pressure

c) Absolute pressure of a liquid must be equal to it's vapor pressure

d) Absolute pressure of a liquid must be greater than it's vapor pressure

12. Which of the following machines have the possibility of cavitation?

a) Reaction turbines and centrifugal pumps

b) Reaction turbines and reciprocating pumps

c) Impulse turbines and centrifugal pumps

d) Impulse turbines and reciprocating pumps

13. The three liquids 1, 2, and 3 with vapor pressures V1, V2 and V3 respectively, are kept under same pressure. If V1 > V2 > V3, which liquid will start boiling early?

a) liquid 1

b) liquid 2

c) liquid 3

d) they will start boiling at the same time

14. Equal amount of a particular liquid is poured into three similar containers, namely 1, 2 and 3, at a temperature of T1, T2 and T3 respectively. If T1 < T2 < T3, the liquid in which container will have the highest vapor pressure?

a) container 1

b) container 2

c) container 3

d) the vapor pressure of the liquid will remain the same irrespective of it's temperature

15. The absolute pressure of a water is 0.5kN above it's vapor pressure. If it flows with a velocity of 1m/s, what will be the value of Cavitation Number describing the flow induced boiling?

a) 0.25

b) 0.5

c) 1

d) 2

16. Which of the following is correct regarding the formation and collapse of vapor bubbles in a liquid?

a) Vapor bubbles are formed when the fluid pressure goes above the vapor pressure and collapses when the fluid pressure goes above the bubble pressure

b) Vapor bubbles are formed when the fluid pressure goes above the vapor pressure and collapses when the fluid pressure goes below the bubble pressure

c) Vapor bubbles are formed when the fluid pressure drops below the vapor pressure and collapses when the fluid pressure goes below the bubble pressure

d) Vapor bubbles are formed when the fluid pressure drops below the vapor pressure and collapses when the fluid pressure goes above the bubble pressure

Hydraulic System MCQ for Structural Engineering

1.Hydraulic energy is converted into another form of energy by hydraulic machines. What form of energy is that?

a) Mechanical Energy

b) Electrical Energy

c) Nuclear Energy

d) Elastic Energy

3. Which principle is used in Hydraulic Turbines?

a) Faraday law

b) Newton's second law

c) Charles law

d) Braggs law

4. Buckets and blades used in a turbine are used to:

a) Alter the direction of water

b) Switch off the turbine

c) To regulate the wind speed

d) To regenerate the power

5. ________________is the electric power obtained from the energy of the water.

a) Roto dynamic power

b) Thermal power

c) Nuclear power

d) Hydroelectric power

6. Which energy generated in a turbine is used to run electric power generator linked to the turbine shaft?

a) Mechanical Energy

b) Potential Energy

c) Elastic Energy

d) Kinetic Energy

7. Hydraulic Machines fall under the category :

a) Pulverizers

b) Kinetic machinery

c) Condensers

d) Roto-dynamic machinery

8.Which kind of turbines changes the pressure of the water entered through it?

A) Reaction turbines

b) Impulse turbines

c) Reactive turbines

d) Kinetic turbines

9. Which type of turbine is used to change the velocity of the water through its flow?

a) Kinetic turbines

b) Axial flow turbines

c) Impulse turbines

d) Reaction turbines

10. Which type of turbine is a Francis Turbine?

a) Impulse Turbine

b) Screw Turbine

c) Reaction turbine

d) Turgo turbine

11.How many types of Reaction turbines are there?

a) 5

b) 4
c) 3
d) 9
13.Which kind of turbine is a Fourneyron Turbine?
a) Inward flow turbine
b) <u>Outward flow turbine</u>
c) Mixed flow turbine
d) Radial flow turbine

www.ingramcontent.com/pod-product-compliance
Ingram Content Group UK Ltd.
Pitfield, Milton Keynes, MK11 3LW, UK
UKHW021921190726
13853UKWH00002B/774

9 798889 091158